THE WORLD'S GREATEST
OLYMPIANS

Michael Hurley

Heinemann
LIBRARY
Chicago, Illinois

www.heinemannraintree.com
Visit our website to find out
more information about
Heinemann-Raintree books.

To order:

☎ Phone 888-454-2279

💻 Visit www.heinemannraintree.com
to browse our catalog and order online.

© 2012 Heinemann Library
an imprint of Capstone Global Library, LLC
Chicago, Illinois

Edited by Kate de Villiers and Laura Knowles
Designed by Richard Parker
Picture research by Liz Alexander
Production by Camilla Crask
Originated by Capstone Global Library Ltd
Printed and bound in China by CTPS

15 14 13 12 11
10 9 8 7 6 5 4 3 2 1

Library of Congress Cataloging-in-Publication Data
Hurley, Michael, 1979-
  The world's greatest Olympians / Michael Hurley.
    p. cm.—(The Olympics)
  Includes bibliographical references and index.
  ISBN 978-1-4109-4122-0 (hb)—ISBN 978-1-4109-4128-2 (pb)
  1. Olympics—History. 2. Athletes—History. I. Title.
  GV721.5.H88 2012
    796.48—dc22   2010049495

Acknowledgments
We would like to thank the following for permission to
reproduce photographs: Corbis pp. **5** (© STAFF/Reuters),
7 (© Hulton-Deutsch Collection), **9** (© Bettmann), **17**
(© Dimitri Iundt/TempSport), **21** (© Paul J Sutton/PCN),
25 (© Kerim Okten/epa), **27** (© Ola Fagerstrom); Getty Images
pp. **11** (Popperfoto), **14** (Mike Powell /Allsport), **19** (Ross
Kinnaird/ALLSPORT), **23** (Eric Feferberg/AFP), **24** (Nicolas
Asfouri/AFP); Press Association Images p. **13** (S&G and
Barratts/EMPICS Sport).

Cover photograph of USA's Michael Johnson celebrating a
gold victory reproduced with permission of Press Association
Images/Tony Marshall/EMPICS Sport.

Every effort has been made to contact copyright holders of
material reproduced in this book. Any omissions will be
rectified in subsequent printings if notice is given to the
publisher.

Contents

Some words are shown in bold, **like this**. You can find them in the glossary on page 30.

Going for Gold

The Olympic Games is an international sports event held every four years. Thousands of athletes representing more than 200 countries take part in various Olympic events.

2012 olympics

The 2012 Olympics will be held in London in the United Kingdom. The city won the right to host the event ahead of other major cities including Paris, France; Madrid, Spain; and New York City.

There are 38 different sports in the Olympics. Athletes compete to be crowned Olympic champion in their chosen sport. Medals are given to the athletes who finish in the top three places: gold for first, silver for second, and bronze for third. Every athlete wants to win an Olympic gold medal. Becoming an Olympic champion makes you famous all over the world.

Ultimate olympian

The most successful athlete in Olympic history is Larissa Latynina. She was a gymnast who competed at three Olympics between 1956 and 1964. Latynina won an incredible eighteen medals: nine gold, five silver, and four bronze.

Amazing achievements

In the history of the Olympics there have been some truly outstanding performances and achievements by athletes. These athletes have become Olympic gold medalists because they trained extremely hard. They have been **dedicated** and determined to succeed.

The greatest Olympic champions rose above **expectation** and pressure to perform to the best of their ability. They achieved their goals in front of huge crowds and television audiences of millions.

U.S. swimmer Michael Phelps broke a 36-year Olympic record by winning eight Gold medals at the 2008 Olympic Games in Beijing. Here he is with all eight medals!

Jesse Owens

Jesse Owens became the first world-famous Olympian when he took part in the 1936 Olympic Games in Berlin, Germany. Owens competed in four events and won four gold medals. He was the first U.S. athlete to win four gold medals at one Olympics.

World record time

In the 100 meters, Owens equaled the Olympic record. He also won gold in the 200 meters. His three jumps in the long jump were all longer than any of the other competitors. His fourth gold medal came in the 4 x 100-meter relay. The U.S. team finished first and set a new world record time of 39.80 seconds. The record stood for the next 20 years.

GOING FOR GOLD

Jesse Owens' achievements were incredible because of where he was competing. The German leader, Adolf Hitler, wanted to use the Berlin Olympics to show that German athletes were the best in the world. He believed that the other athletes were **inferior**. Owens's four gold medals proved that Hitler was wrong.

Jesse Owens set a new long-jump world record at the 1936 Berlin Olympics.

Olympic fact file

Name: Jesse Owens
Born: 1913, Oakville, Alabama
Events: 100 meters, 200 meters, 4 x 100-meter relay,
         long jump
Medals: Four gold
Fact: In 1984 the street outside the Berlin Olympic
         stadium was renamed Jesse-Owens-Allee
         (Jesse-Owens-Boulevard).

Fanny Blankers-Koen

At the 1948 London Olympics, 30-year-old Fanny Blankers-Koen became the first female athlete to win four gold medals at one Olympic Games. Her feat was truly remarkable.

First Olympics

Blankers-Koen took part in the 1936 Olympics. She finished in joint sixth place in the high jump and was part of the Dutch 100-meter relay team that finished fifth. During World War II (1939–1945) there were no international athletics events. Blankers-Koen continued to train and compete in her homeland of Holland.

Winning gold

In 1948 Blankers-Koen wanted to take part in **multiple** events, including the high jump and the long jump. She was already the world-record holder in these events. Blankers-Koen was restricted by Olympic rules to three individual events. She chose to compete in the 100 meters, 200 meters, and 80-meter hurdles. She won all three events. Her fourth gold medal came as part of the Dutch relay team.

Olympic fact file

Name: Fanny Blankers-Koen
Born: 1918, Baarn, Netherlands
Events: 100 meters, 200 meters, 4 x 100-meter relay, 80-meter hurdles
Medals: Four gold
Fact: Blankers-Koen was nicknamed "the flying Dutch housewife."

In the 1940s it was very unusual for a 30-year-old housewife with children, such as Fanny Blankers-Koen, to become a world-class athlete.

Abebe Bikila

Abebe Bikila was an outstanding **marathon** runner. He was the first person to win the Olympic marathon twice. He won gold in 1960 in Rome, Italy, and repeated this achievement four years later at the 1964 Olympics in Tokyo, Japan.

Running barefoot

Bikila took part in his first Olympic Games in 1960. He was used to training at home in Ethiopia, in Africa, without any shoes. Amazingly, he ran like this in the Olympics. He was not one of the favorites to win, but he ended up breaking the world and Olympic marathon records. During the marathon he kept up with the front-runners, and with one mile to go he raced into the lead. Bikila won the race by 25 seconds.

Olympic fact file

Name: Abebe Bikila
Born: 1932, Mont, Ethiopia
Event: Marathon
Medals: Two gold
Fact: Bikila was the first African to win an Olympic gold medal.

Here, Abebe Bikila—running barefoot—is on his way to winning gold in the marathon event in Rome in 1960.

Remarkable triumph

Bikila's second Olympic marathon triumph was incredible. Just six weeks before the 1964 Olympics, he had to have an emergency operation to remove his **appendix**. This meant that he could not train at all. Astonishingly, after 22 miles (35.4 kilometers) of the race, he was over 2 miles (3.2 kilometers) ahead of his nearest rival. He won the race easily.

Carl Lewis

Carl Lewis is one of the greatest and most recognizable athletes of the 20th century. He is also one of the most famous athletes in Olympic history. During an outstanding career that included four Olympics, the U.S. athlete won an amazing total of nine gold medals and one silver medal. In his first Olympics, in 1984 in Los Angeles, California, Lewis matched Jesse Owens's record of four gold medals. Lewis won the 100 meters, 200 meters, 4 x 100-meter relay, and the long jump.

Second Olympics

At the 1988 Olympics, Lewis was at the center of a **scandal** after the 100-meter final. He had been beaten into second place by the Canadian sprinter, Ben Johnson. However, a few days after the final, Johnson was stripped of his gold medal. He tested positive for **performance-enhancing drugs** and was **disqualified**. Lewis was named the 100 meters Olympic champion.

Comparing Jesse Owens and Carl Lewis

Athlete	100 meters	200 meters	Long jump
Jesse Owens (1936)	10.30 seconds	20.70 seconds	8 meters, 6 centimeters (26 ft, 5 in)
Carl Lewis (1984)	9.99 seconds	19.80 seconds	8 meters, 54 centimeters (28 ft)

Carl Lewis was named World Athlete of the Year three times between 1982 and 1984. In 1999 he was named Olympic Athlete of the Century by the International Association of Athletics Federation (IAAF).

Olympic fact file

Name: Frederick Carlton Lewis
Born: 1961, Birmingham, Alabama
Events: 100 meters, 200 meters, 4 x 100-meter relay, long jump
Medals: Nine gold, one silver
Fact: Lewis was nicknamed "King Carl"

Michael Johnson

United States athlete Michael Johnson is the only man to win gold in the 200 meters and 400 meters at the same Olympics. Johnson is also the only male athlete to win gold in the 400 meters at **consecutive** Olympics.

Stopped in his tracks

At the 1992 Olympics in Barcelona, Spain, Johnson was expected to compete for gold in the 200 and 400 meters. During the Games Johnson was struck with food poisoning and he could not take part in the final of either event. He recovered enough to help his teammates win the 4 x 400-meter relay.

Michael Johnson stood out from the other track athletes. He wore special gold running shoes. He also had an unusual, upright running style.

Battling back

Johnson overcame the disappointment of Barcelona four years later in Atlanta, Georgia. He won the 400 meters with a new Olympic record of 43.49 seconds. Three days later, the pressure was on to complete a gold-medal double by winning the 200 meters. He smashed the world record and won gold. His winning time of 19.32 seconds would remain the unbeaten world record for more than ten years. Four years later, Johnson won the 400 meters Olympic title again.

Olympic fact file

Name: Michael Johnson
Born: 1967, Dallas, Texas
Events: 200 meters, 400 meters, 4 x 400-meter relay
Medals: Five gold
Fact: Johnson returned one of his gold medals after it became clear that another member of the winning 4 x 400-meter U.S. relay team in 2000 had used **performance-enhancing drugs**.

Cathy Freeman

At the Olympic Games in 2000, in Sydney, Australia, Cathy Freeman was under a lot of pressure to win gold in the 400 meters. This was because the Olympics were being held in her own country. She was also the favorite to win the race.

Special honor

When the Sydney Olympics started, Freeman was invited to light the Olympic torch at the opening ceremony. It was the first time that an athlete competing in the Olympics had been given this honor.

The hopes of a nation

As the athletes lined up for the 400-meter final, all eyes were on Freeman in the stadium—and on television screens all over the world. She wore a special suit, with a tight-fitting hood, in the Australian sporting colors of green and gold. Freeman coped well under the intense pressure and managed to win the race convincingly. After the race Freeman said, "I was very incredibly happy, but more than anything I was relieved."

Olympic fact file

Name: Cathy Freeman
Born: 1973, Mackay, Queensland, Australia
Event: 400 meters
Medals: One gold, one silver
Fact: Freeman was the first **Aboriginal**-Australian female athlete to compete at the Olympics when she took part in the 400 meters in 1992

Cathy Freeman is pictured during the heats for the 400 meters in 2000. She went on to win gold in the final.

Steve Redgrave

The Englishman Steve Redgrave is one of the most successful athletes in Olympic history. He competed in five **consecutive** Olympics over a period of twenty years and won a gold medal each time! He won his first gold medal as part of a four-man rowing team at the Los Angeles Olympic Games in 1984.

Unbeatable combination

At the next Olympics in Seoul, South Korea, in 1988, Redgrave was part of a two-man crew that won gold. He then began rowing alongside Matthew Pinsent, who was a strong and powerful rower. The pair became world famous. They were unbeatable, winning gold at the 1992 and 1996 Olympics. Redgrave finished his Olympic career in the same way he had started. He won a gold medal as part of a four-man rowing team at the 2000 Olympic Games in Sydney, Australia.

A true inspiration

Redgrave was **diagnosed** with **diabetes** three years before his final Olympic appearance. He had to adapt his lifestyle and training to cope with his condition. He did not let diabetes stop him from competing and succeeding at the highest level. Redgrave has been an inspiration to many people who suffer from the condition.

Steve Redgrave in action during the 2000 Olympics, in Sydney. He won his fifth gold medal with the help of his crew, Mathew Pinsent, Tim Foster, and James Cracknell.

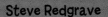

Steve Redgrave

Olympic fact file

Name: Steve Redgrave
Born: 1962, Marlow, Buckinghamshire, UK
Sport: Rowing
Medals: Five gold, one bronze
Fact: The British queen **knighted** Redgrave in 2001 in recognition of his amazing Olympic feats. He became Sir Steven Redgrave.

Michael Phelps

United States swimmer Michael Phelps is the most successful male athlete in Olympic history. In two Olympic Games he managed to win fourteen gold and two bronze medals. Phelps began his record medal haul at the 2004 Olympics in Athens, Greece. He competed in eight different swimming races and won six. He finished third in the others, one of which was a team relay.

A massive challenge

At the 2008 Olympics in Beijing, China, Phelps aimed to win eight gold medals. No one had done this before. Another U.S. swimmer, Mark Spitz, managed to win seven in 1972. Phelps won his first seven races, including three team relays, and the pressure started to grow. The crowds grew as spectators hoped to see history being made. In one of the closest finishes in Olympic history, Phelps then won the 100-meter **butterfly** by 0.01 second!

GOING FOR GOLD

Michael Phelps has the perfect physique to be a successful swimmer. He is 6 feet 4 inches (1.93 meters) tall, and his arms span over 6 1/2 feet (2 meters). He has a long **torso** and size 14 feet. These physical characteristics help him power through the water.

Olympic fact file

Name: Michael Phelps
Born: 1985, Baltimore, Maryland
Sport: Swimming
Medals: Fourteen gold, two bronze
Fact: Phelps set seven world records at the 2008 Olympics.

Here, Michael Phelps is in action in the 200-meter butterfly race at the 2008 Olympics. He won the race and set a new world record.

Michael Phelps's Olympic record

2008 Olympics	Medal	Record
400-meter **individual medley**	gold	world record
4 x 100-meter freestyle relay	gold	world record
200-meter freestyle	gold	world record
200-meter butterfly	gold	world record
4 x 200-meter freestyle relay	gold	world record
200-meter individual medley	gold	world record
4 x 100-meter medley relay	gold	world record
100-meter butterfly	gold	Olympic record

Yelena Isinbaeva

In 2004 Russian pole-vaulter Yelena Isinbaeva won her first Olympic gold medal at the Olympic Games in Athens, Greece. She set a new Olympic record height of 16 feet, 1½ inches (4.91 meters) for the women's pole vault. Four years later in Beijing, China, Isinbaeva won the gold medal in the pole vault again. This time she set a new world record, and vaulted more than 7⅘ inches (20 centimeters) higher than her closest competitor.

Choosing a different sport

When she was fifteen years old, Isinbaeva had to give up on a career as a gymnast because she had grown too tall. She has dominated the women's pole vault ever since she started competing. The strength that she gained from gymnastics together with her height helped to make the pole vault the ideal event for her. She was the first woman to vault more than 5 meters (16 feet, 4 inches).

Pole vault history

The Olympic pole vault event for men has taken place since the first modern Olympics in 1896. The first Olympic pole vault for women did not take place until 2000.

Olympic fact file

Name: Yelena Isinbaeva
Born: 1982, Volgograd, Russia
Event: Pole vault
Medals: Two gold
Fact: Isinbaeva has broken the women's pole
          vault world record 16 times!

Usain Bolt

Jamaican sprinter Usain ("Lightning") Bolt became the fastest man in the world at the 2008 Olympic Games in Beijing, China. He won the gold medal in the 100-meter sprint with a new world record time. Bolt won three gold medals in total at the Beijing Olympics. He added to his 100 meters gold with success in the 200 meters and the 4 x 100-meter relay.

Pressure to perform

Usain Bolt is always under a lot of pressure to win convincingly. He does not appear to let the pressure affect him. Before a race he seems very relaxed as he dances and waves to the crowd.

Here, Usain Bolt is winning the 100 meters. He was so far ahead of his opponents that he slowed down at the finish!

Olympic fact file

Name: Usain Bolt
Born: 1986, Montego Bay, Jamaica
Events: 100 meters, 200 meters, 4 x 100-meter relay
Medals: Three gold
Fact: Bolt holds the world record for 100 meters at 9.58 seconds.

Comparing sprint times

Athlete	Year	100 meters	200 meters
Jesse Owens	1932	10.30 seconds	20.70 seconds
Carl Lewis	1984	9.99 seconds	19.80 seconds
Michael Johnson	1996	N/A	19.32 seconds
Usain Bolt	2008	9.69 seconds	19.30 seconds

Chris Hoy

At the 2008 Olympic Games in Beijing, China, the cyclist Chris Hoy became the first British athlete in one hundred years to win three gold medals. This was an outstanding achievement. Hoy had taken part in two previous Olympics. He won a silver medal in a team cycling event in Sydney, Australia, in 2000. He also won an individual gold medal in Athens, Greece, in 2004.

Record achievement

Hoy was one of the favorites to win a gold medal at the Beijing Olympics, but no one expected him to win three. He won two individual gold medals, and he helped his teammates to win another. Hoy also broke two world records in Beijing.

Olympic fact file

Name: Chris Hoy
Born: 1976, Edinburgh, Scotland, UK
Sport: Cycling
Medals: Four gold, one silver
Fact: Chris Hoy is the most successful male cyclist in Olympic history. In honor of his great sporting achievements, the British queen **knighted** Hoy in 2008. He became Sir Christopher Hoy.

GOING FOR GOLD

Chris Hoy is a very powerful cyclist with tremendous strength and **stamina**. He has the speed to race in the sprint events and can also compete in the long distance, **endurance** events.

Winter and Paralympic Greats

Winter Olympics fact files

The Winter Olympics are held every four years, two years after the Summer Olympics. Here are a few of the greatest Winter Olympic gold medallists:

Name: Lydiya Skoblikova
Born: 1932, Zlatoust, Russia
Sport: Ice skating
Medals: Seven gold
Fact: Skoblikova was the first female Winter Olympic athlete to win four gold medals at one Olympics.

Name: Georg Hackl
Born: 1966, Berchtesgaden, Germany
Sport: **Luge**
Medals: Three gold, two silver
Fact: Hackl competed in five **consecutive** Winter Olympics.

Name: Janica Kostelic
Born: 1982, Zagreb, Croatia
Sport: Skiing
Medals: Four gold, two silver
Fact: Kostelic was the first female athlete to win four skiing medals at one Winter Olympics: three gold and one silver.

Paralympics fact files

The Paralympics follow the Summer Olympic Games every four years. The Paralympics are for athletes who have some form of disability. Here are some of the greatest Paralympic athletes:

Name: Ragnhild Myklebust
Born: 1943, Oslo, Norway
Events: **Biathlon**, cross-country skiing
Medals: Seventeen gold, three silver, two bronze
Fact: Myklbust is the most successful athlete in the history of the Paralympics.

Name: Arnold Boldt
Born: 1957, Osler, Saskatchewan, Canada
Events: Standing high jump and standing long jump
Medals: Seven gold, two silver
Fact: Boldt was named the "Outstanding performer of the games" at the 1976 Toronto Paralympics.

Name: Tanni Grey-Thompson
Born: 1969, Cardiff, United Kingdom
Sport: Wheelchair racing
Medals: Eleven gold, three silver, one bronze
Fact: Grey-Thompson won four gold medals at both the 1992 and 2000 Paralympics.

Glossary

Aboriginal original people of Australia. Aboriginal people lived in Australia for more than 45,000 years before settlers arrived from Europe.

appendix part of the human digestive system that can be removed without causing problems

biathlon winter sport that involves cross-country skiing and rifle shooting

butterfly type of swimming stroke. The swimmer moves both arms over the head at the same time and kicks both feet to move through the water.

consecutive following one another in order

dedicated completely committed to something

diabetes condition that leads to too much glucose (sugar) in the blood

diagnose understand the cause of an illness or condition after tests and examinations

disqualify stop someone from being part of a race or competition because they have broken the rules

endurance type of race that lasts a long time

expectation waiting for something to happen

individual medley type of swimming race. It includes swimming lengths of freestyle, breaststroke, butterfly, and back crawl.

inferior lower in quality or value

knighted given the title "Sir" by the British monarch

luge Winter Olympic sport that involves lying flat on a sled and sliding down a track

marathon long running race held over 26.2 miles (42.2 kilometers)

multiple more than one

performance-enhancing drug substance that is taken illegally to make an athlete faster and stronger

scandal event that causes public outrage

stamina ability to do something for a long time

torso top half of the human body

Find Out More

Books

Christopher, Matt. *The Olympics: Legendary Sports Events*. New York: Little, Brown Books for Young Readers, 2008.

Macy, Sue. *Swifter, Higher, Stronger: A Photographic History of the Summer Olympics*. Washington, D.C.: National Geographic Children's Books, 2008.

Zuehlke, Jeffrey. *Michael Phelps*. Minneapolis: Lerner Publications, 2009.

Websites

www.carllewis.com
This website tells the story of Carl Lewis's childhood and his successful athletic career.

www.cathyfreeman.com.au
This is the official website for Australian athlete Cathy Freeman.

www.chrishoy.com
Visit this website to learn more about Olympic cyclist Chris Hoy.

www.olympic.org
The official website of the International Olympic Committee includes facts and statistics about all the Olympic Games and medal winners.

www.paralympic.org
This is the official website of the Paralympic movement.

www.steveredgrave.com
Visit Steve Redgrave's official website to find out more about his amazing rowing career.

www.yelenaisinbaeva.com
Go to this website to find out more about record-breaking Olympic pole-vaulter Yelena Isinbaeva.

Index

FEB 0 1 2012